Date: 9/25/12

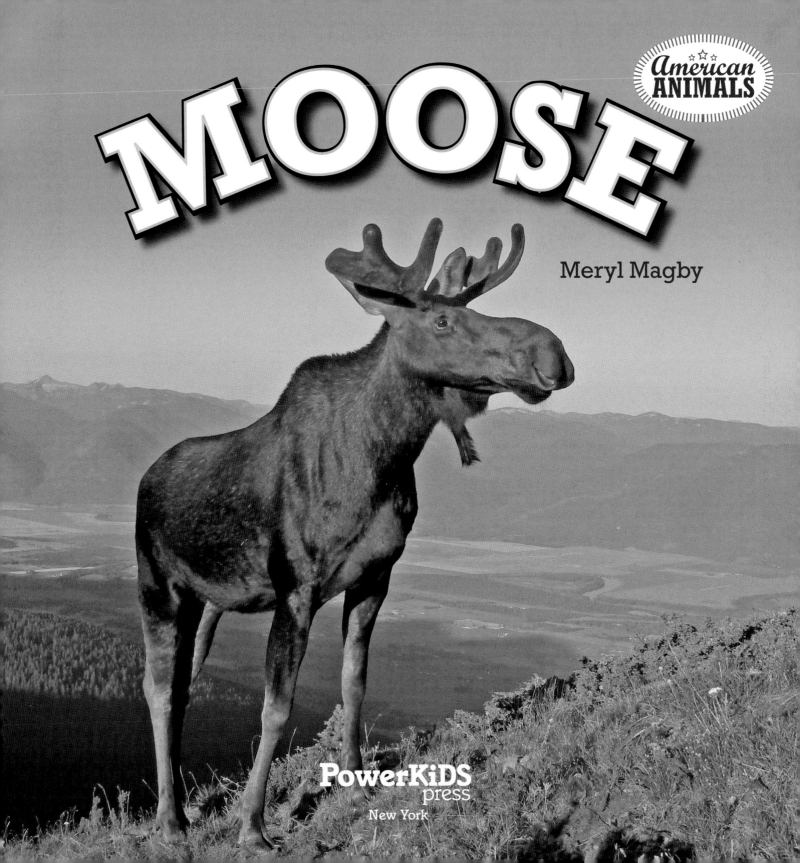

MOOSE

American ANIMALS

Meryl Magby

PowerKiDS press

New York

Published in 2012 by The Rosen Publishing Group, Inc.
29 East 21st Street, New York, NY 10010

First Edition

Editor: Amelie von Zumbusch
Book Design: Ashley Drago

Photo Credits: Cover, pp. 4, 5, 7 (top, bottom), 10, 11, 16, 19, 20, 21 (top) Shutterstock.com; p. 6 Jupiterimages/Liquidlibrary/Thinkstock; pp. 8–9 Jeff Foott/Getty Images; pp. 12–13 Purestock/Getty Images; p. 14 Hemera/Thinkstock; p. 15 © Milo Burcham/age fotostock; p. 17 (right) Visuals Unlimited, Inc./Joe McDonald/Getty Images; p. 17 (left) © www.iStockphoto.com/Bradley L. Marlow; p. 18 iStockphoto/Thinkstock; p. 21 (bottom) Tom Brakefield/Stockbyte/Thinkstock; p. 22 Jochen Schlenker/ Getty Images.

Library of Congress Cataloging-in-Publication Data

Magby, Meryl.
 Moose / by Meryl Magby. — 1st ed.
    p. cm. — (American animals)
 ISBN 978-1-4488-6183-5 (library binding) — ISBN 978-1-4488-6325-9 (pbk.) —
 ISBN 978-1-4488-6326-6 (6-pack)
 1. Moose—Juvenile literature. I. Title.
 QL737.U55.M274 2012
 599.65'7—dc23
                                        2011029061

Manufactured in the United States of America

CPSIA Compliance Information: Batch #WW12PK: For Further Information contact Rosen Publishing, New York, New York at 1-800-237-9932

Contents

Moose in North America

Male moose, such as this one, often measure 6 feet (2 m) tall, from their feet to their shoulders.

Moose are the largest members of the deer family. They are also one of the largest land **mammals** in North America. Some people say that moose look like a mix of a hippo and a horse! Male moose are famous for their large **antlers**.

Moose live in the United States and Canada. They also live in parts of northern Europe and Asia, where they are called elk. For many years, moose disappeared from parts of the northeastern United States. This happened because their **habitats**, or homes, were being destroyed. Today, moose **populations** are growing. These big animals can be found in the Northeast again.

This is a female moose. Unlike males, female moose do not generally grow antlers.

Moose Bodies

Moose have long, thick fur. Their fur may be brown or black.

Moose have large bodies and heads. They have humps on their shoulders. Their legs are long and thin. Moose's front legs are longer than their back legs. This helps them jump easily. Like other members of the deer family, moose have hooves.

Male moose are called bulls. Bulls have large antlers for much of the year. Moose have flaps of skin that hang under their chins, called bells. Males have much larger bells than females do. Bulls weigh between 600 and 1,600 pounds (270–725 kg). Adult females, or cows, can weigh as much as 800 pounds (360 kg).

Moose are known for their long, wide noses. Their noses make it easy to tell moose apart from other members of the deer family.

A bull's antlers may grow to be more than 5 feet (1.5 m) wide. They can weigh more than 60 pounds (27 kg).

Forests and Wetlands

Moose can be found in every Canadian province and territory. In the United States, they are found in New England, the Rocky Mountains, and around the Great Lakes.

> This moose is in the woods of Maine. Maine is home to more than 25,000 moose. The moose is the state animal of Maine.

Moose like to live in forests where there are also lakes, wetlands, or **marshes**. They will live in areas where the forest has been cut or burned down and new plants are beginning to grow, too. In the summer, moose look for wet, shady places to stay cool. In the winter, they move to areas where the snow does not get too high. They may also move to different areas to **mate** and have babies.

Hungry Plant Eaters

Moose eat the leaves of many trees, such as willows, birches, aspens, sugar maples, and mountain ashes.

Moose eat plants. They eat the leaves, twigs, and buds of trees and shrubs that grow in their forest habitats. They will also eat other plants, such as grasses, **lichen**, moss, and mushrooms.

In the cold winter months, moose strip the bark from trees with their teeth and

This moose is eating lily pads in Wyoming's Grand Teton National Park. Lily pads are one of several aquatic plants that moose eat.

eat it. In the summer, moose also like to eat **aquatic** plants that grow in ponds or wetlands. The moose wade into the water and will even stick their heads under the surface to reach the plants. Eating these plants is also a good way for moose to get salt in their **diets**.

Moose Facts

1. Moose can eat between 40 and 60 pounds (18–27 kg) of food a day. They can store more than 100 pounds (45 kg) of food in their stomachs.

4. Moose can move their ears in different directions at the same time. They can also do this with their eyes. This lets moose listen and watch for danger more easily.

2. Moose are good swimmers. They learn to swim when they are just a few weeks old.

3. Moose tracks are heart shaped. The tracks are between 4 and 6 inches (10–15 cm) long and 3.5 to 6 inches (9–15 cm) wide.

5. The Algonquin peoples gave moose their name. The word "moose" comes from an Algonquin word that means "twig eater."

6. Moose are not **aggressive** animals. However, they can become a danger to people when they are hungry, tired after walking through snow, or being bothered by people, dogs, or cars.

7. Moose that live in Europe and Asia are called elk. In the United States, the name "elk" is used for a different member of the deer family. This relative of the moose is also known as the wapiti.

8. When bugs bother them, moose may lower their whole bodies into the water. Moose also roll in mud when there are a lot of bugs. Bugs are less likely to bite a moose when it is covered in mud.

How Moose Live

Though many American animals live in large groups, adult moose most often live alone. However, cows and their babies stay together throughout the year until the babies are old enough to live on their own. Moose are most active during the daytime. At night, they sleep on the ground. This leaves large dents in the grass or the snow.

Male moose, such as this one, spend most of their time alone.

Before they mate, a cow and bull may nuzzle, or rub their noses together, as this pair is doing.

Each fall, bulls and cows look for mates. The mating season, or rut, starts each September. During this time, bulls fight to decide which ones will mate with cows. Cows make noises to let bulls know they are ready to mate.

New Antlers Every Year

Some bulls fight very aggressively, others less so.

Bull moose begin to grow their antlers each March or April. Their antlers have a soft, furry covering, called velvet. The bulls' antlers reach their full size by late summer. Calves and younger bulls tend to grow much smaller antlers than full-grown bulls do.

Bulls start scraping the velvet off their antlers at the end of the summer. They do this by rubbing their antlers against trees and shrubs. During the mating season, in September and October, bulls fight each other and knock their antlers together. They generally shed their antlers between November and January, after the mating season is over.

This moose is losing the velvet on its antlers. You can see strips of velvet hanging from its antlers.

This moose is in velvet. That means that the velvet is still covering its antlers. A moose's antlers have velvet on them while they are growing.

Growing Up

Moose calves weigh between 20 and 25 pounds (9–11 kg) when they are born. Their fur is a reddish-brown color.

Cows tend to have their babies in May or June. Baby moose are called calves. Moose calves can stand up within a few hours of being born. They walk soon after that. Calves drink their mothers' milk for about six months. This helps them grow strong. By fall, the calves weigh about 300 to 400 pounds (136–181 kg).

A calf will stay with its mother until she gives birth to a new calf the following spring. Then, the young moose starts out on its own. The **life span** of a moose tends to be about 15 years in the wild.

> Cows often have only one baby. They may have twins if they have had enough food to eat during the last year, though.

Predators and People

Many of the states where moose live have laws that limit how many moose can be killed by hunters each year.

Black bears and coyotes often hunt moose calves. Calves are not as fast or strong as adult moose. This makes it easier for **predators** to catch them. However, cow moose often make loud noises and stomp their feet to scare predators away from their calves. Adult moose have predators, too. Cougars, gray wolves, and grizzly bears hunt

full-grown moose. Bulls may be able to fight off predators with their antlers or outrun them.

People also hunt moose. Moose hunting is a popular sport in the northern states with large moose populations. Many people also kill moose by mistake by hitting them with their cars.

Wolves hunt in groups, called packs. The members of a pack work together. This makes it easier for them to hunt big animals, such as moose.

Grizzly bears live in northwestern North America. While they sometimes eat big animals, such as moose, grizzlies eat mainly smaller animals and plants.

Moose Today

Today, scientists are still learning about how moose live. Some scientists study moose with the help of **radio collars**. These tools let scientists follow moose's movements throughout the year.

Moose live in many national parks and wildlife **refuges**, such as the Arctic National Wildlife Refuge, in Alaska, and Yellowstone National Park, in Wyoming, Idaho, and Montana. The US government watches over these places. National parks and wildlife refuges will be safe places for moose to live for years to come.

This moose lives in Alaska's Denali National Park and Preserve.

Glossary

aggressive (uh-GREH-siv) Ready to fight.

antlers (ANT-lerz) Large branchlike horns that grow on the heads of some animals.

aquatic (uh-KWAH-tik) Living or growing in water.

diets (DY-uts) Food that animals normally eat.

habitats (HA-buh-tats) The kinds of land where animals or plants naturally live.

lichen (LY-ken) Living things that are made of two kinds of living things, called algae and fungi.

life span (LYF SPAN) The amount of time that something is alive.

mammals (MA-mulz) Warm-blooded animals that have backbones and hair, breathe air, and feed milk to their young.

marshes (MAHRSH-ez) Areas of soft, wet land.

mate (MAYT) To come together to make babies.

populations (pop-yoo-LAY-shunz) Groups of animals or people living in the same place.

predators (PREH-duh-terz) Animals that kill other animals for food.

radio collars (RAY-dee-oh KAH-lerz) Things that scientists put around animals' necks to track their movements.

refuges (REH-fyoo-jez) Places where things are kept safe.

Index

A

antlers, 4, 7, 16–17, 21

Asia, 5, 13

B

babies, 8, 14, 18

E

elk, 5, 13

Europe, 5, 13

H

habitats, 5, 10

heads, 6, 11

hippo, 4

homes, 5

horse, 4

humps, 6

L

lichen, 10

life span, 19

M

mammals, 4

marshes, 8

P

people(s), 4, 13, 21

populations, 5, 21

R

radio collars, 22

refuge(s), 22

Web Sites

Due to the changing nature of Internet links, PowerKids Press has developed an online list of Web sites related to the subject of this book. This site is updated regularly. Please use this link to access the list:

www.powerkidslinks.com/aman/moose/